The Satir Approach
to Communication

The Satir Approach to Communication

A WORKSHOP LEADER'S MANUAL

by
Johanna Schwab
and
Michele Baldwin
Jane Gerber
Maria Gomori
Virginia Satir

SCIENCE AND BEHAVIOR BOOKS
Palo Alto, California

Library of Congress Card Number: 89-061218

ISBN: 8314-0071-4

Illustrations by Barry Ives
Cover design by Anne Marie Rossi
Editing and interior design by Rain Blockley
Typesetting by TLC Graphics
Printed in the United States of America by
    Haddon Craftsmen

We want to acknowledge and extend our
appreciation to the late
Virginia Satir
for creating the many learning opportunities
without which this manual could never have
been compiled.

It is with deepest gratitude that we dedicate this
manual to her.

Michele Baldwin ◊ Jane Gerber ◊ Maria Gomori ◊ Johanna Schwab
Members of the Avanta Network

Contents

Preface

This manual presents a focused training program on human communication. Its material applies to persons—professionals and nonprofessionals alike. The aim is to create a process and develop skills so that each individual can become more fully empowered.

Communication is to personal health, satisfactory interpersonal relationships, and productivity as breathing is to life. Effective communication can be both taught and learned. We were not born with the way we communicate. We learned it, mostly through modeling, in ways no one even knew or intended.

This program is built around the concepts of communication developed by me. Care is taken so that the program's context and process are consistent with those concepts of communication.

This workshop program is basically geared to twenty-four hours of presentation, which can be divided to suit a particular context (for example, two twelve-hour segments, or four six-hour segments). It can be adapted to a longer time span as well. Group size can vary from 6 people to 102, to accommodate units of 2 and 3 persons. Workshop size also depends on the comfort, confidence, courage, and creativity of the leader or leaders.

This program is predicated on the following basic assumptions:

◇ Communication can be meaningful and congruent, with the result that the relationships can be nourishing and supportive.

◇ People have inner resources which they can use more creatively so that their communication can be congruent.

◇ In a workshop format, people can learn new communication patterns through self-awareness and self-understanding.

Have an enlightening, fun time learning.

—Virginia Satir

Part I.
General
Guidelines

Introduction

The guidelines in this book are to help you lead, facilitate, produce, or conduct communication workshops. This manual is designed for persons who have had experiences with Virginia Satir and are familiar with her process.

It is intended to be a blueprint. It is a way to go, not a how-to-do-it manual. We are not suggesting that these are the only ways to present these exercises and experiences. Nor do we want to exclude your own creative innovations. We mean to help you meet the needs of any particular group with whom you are working.

This guide reflects the ways in which Virginia Satir works with people. We have drawn on our observations, experiences, and learnings from participating and training with her since 1962. We describe some of her concepts, ideas, and techniques as well as the ways we have personalized them in our own communication workshops.

Our experiences with groups and with Virginia Satir have shown us that people are eager to develop more human and rewarding ways of relating to each other. Communication skills help people expand their capacities for creating more meaningful and satisfying relationships, both personal and professional. This program therefore sets aside a time and place to focus on *how* we talk to one another and to become aware that:

◇ How we communicate can affect how we feel about ourselves, each other, and our current situation.

◇ Our feelings affect our communication.

◇ We have thoughts, feelings, and body responses at any moment, and we express them differently under differing conditions.

◇ We react to the ways others express their feelings, thoughts, and body sensations.

To promote these awarenesses, Virginia has developed various experiential exercises. These are only a part of any communication workshop. To build an integrated experience, we have applied each of these learning modalities:

◊ **The intellectual:** using didactic information

◊ **The visual:** using demonstrations, charts, diagrams, and videotapes, with the facilitator portraying congruent communication

◊ **The auditory:** using audiotapes, having discussions, and voicing responses to the workshop exercises

◊ **The kinesthetic:** role-playing and using the body to sculpt communication stances

◊ **The experiential:** participating in the exercises and vignettes

Administrative
Details

As soon as you contact an organizer or sponsor
to give a communication workshop or a series, it's
valuable to begin a diary or journal. Start with
your ideas, and your meeting with the organizer,
and continue through the end of the workshop,
including debriefing and evaluation.

PRELIMINARY DETAILS

After making contact, these details need attention:

◊ Name, address, and phone number of
person in charge

◇ Date, time, address, and phone number of workshop location

◇ The number of participants expected and their general background

◇ Your responsibilities

◇ The responsibilities of the organizer

◇ Financial details: fees, expenses, who pays and when

◇ The expectations of the organizer

◇ Your expectations, general ideas, and plans for the program

◇ Logistics for transportation, housing, meals, etc.

◇ Information as to the physical layout of the workshop site, including wheelchair accessibility, and any special needs to make the place adequate and comfortable (The essentials are good lighting, good ventilation, movable chairs, and simple refreshments.)

◇ The equipment you are requesting from the organizer: flip charts, mikes, etc. (see Appendix 3)

◇ Copies of any ads, announcements, or brochures

◇ Sign-up sheets for your mailing list

◇ Evaluation forms

Any contractual agreement between you and the organizer must be in writing, whether informally by letter or in a legal contract.

If you will be working with another person, or several, it's imperative that you explore your personal vulnerabilities and perceptions and expectations of yourself, each other, and the workshop. This processing leads to a trust that is basic to a successful learning experience for you, your partners, and the workshop participants.

YOUR ROLE AS FACILITATOR

The way you communicate as you conduct the workshop is one of your most powerful tools for teaching others. Perfection is not the point; how you handle normal, everyday glitches in communication is as important as the way you portray ideal interaction. Overall, your role is:

To model congruent communication,
being clear, distinct, and direct

To listen carefully

To practice the Five Freedoms (see
Appendix 2)

To check out how you are being heard

To ask for information when things
are not clear

To give messages in words that match
your affect

To be sensitive to the group's comfort
level and to the program's pacing
and timing

To weave from a specific to a universal
by generalizing

To move from the familiar and less
risk-taking to the newer and less
familiar

To have patience

To use metaphors and images as an
aid to translate strangeness into
familiarity

To implant growth messages whenever
possible

To use every intervention as an
opportunity to enhance participants'
self-esteem

To make statements and responses
in terms that are educational rather than
therapeutic; to focus on learning and
growth

To move slowly and build step by
step so that each experience illustrates
and elaborates a communication
concept

To give everyone the opportunity
to express his or her opinions during
a discussion

To model how differentness and
uniqueness can be used creatively

To use reality as the basis of decision-
making rather than who's right or
who has the power

To translate any request for problem-
solving into process

To use all the methods by which
people learn: didactic, visual, auditory,
experiential, kinesthetic

To avoid questions beginning with "Why?"

To recognize that everyone will not always want or be able to respond to your questions at all times (As another way to emphasize a point or elicit feelings, you may want to say you are asking a rhetorical question.)

To make direct contact with each person, as soon and as frequently as possible—by using the person's name, being at eye level, and being within seeing and hearing distance

To use humor and a light touch

To "knock on the door," meaning that when you ask people to participate, you begin by asking if they are willing to do something new (After completing the experience, inquire how they felt about what they did.)

To reframe words and statements that are negative, indefinite, or unclear

To be alert to nonverbal clues and to check them out for clarity and understanding

To acknowledge and respect pain when it occurs

To be alert to any internal clues that you are veering from your center or are out of balance, and to recenter yourself

To be aware that strength, good will, hope, and humor are present, though not always evident

To know that by staying with the process, you can use yourself, your resources, and those of the group for your mutual growth

To take what has been useful and leave behind what has not, and to learn from both

CONCLUDING DETAILS

At the conclusion of a workshop, check these or any other administrative details that need attention:

◊ If evaluations have been used, collect and send them to the appropriate person

◊ Return any borrowed equipment

◇ If you have kept an attendance record,
 give that to appropriate person; keep a
 mailing list for yourself

◇ Collect any leftover brochures, printouts,
 etc. you have brought

◇ Send your billing statement with receipts
 of expenses to the organizer

◇ If you have been a part of a dyad or triad
 in presenting the workshop, plan for time to
 process your experiences

◇ If you have presented alone, ask that a
 colleague help process with you

◇ If you have kept a journal, enter a final
 evaluation ad analysis of your experience

The Workshop
Process

Communication allows us to make meaning with others and to get our needs met. It is what we use in the intimate art of daily living with others.

There is a significant connection between how a person communicates and the level of his or her self-esteem. Communication styles also affect how creatively and productively we manage our relationships, handle everyday human problems, and develop our own unique capabilities.

This communication workshop involves detailed, step-by-step learnings about each aspect of communication. It increases people's sensitivity to and awareness of how they give out messages: with words, body reactions, and behavior.

Communication is both verbal and nonverbal. Words are not the sole conveyors of messages: the

tone of voice, facial and body movements, and
physical changes also send out messages and are
therefore included in the study of communication.
Communication begins at the very start of the
workshop with your own communication to the
group as to what's going on, information about
the place, and so forth.

Our focus on communication is based on Virginia
Satir's belief that in any learned activity, change
is possible. People create the possibility for change
by learning new ways. Speech is a learned activity,
for instance, so we can transform any patterns
of speech that are no longer fitting into new
learnings. The springboard to more productive
ways is becoming aware of how we handle our
communication.

Throughout this workshop, the thrust is to help
people become increasingly aware of how they are
expressing themselves; the actual words they
are using; how clearly, directly, and specifically
they are communicating, verbally and nonverbally;
and how clearly they are distinguishing between
thoughts, feelings, and body reactions.

This helps people understand how they handle
discrepancies between what was said and what
was intended. It also illuminates how their feelings,
expressed or not, affect their feelings about
themselves, their self-esteem, their feelings about
the other person in a dialogue, and their
relationship with that person, whatever it is.

Ultimately, they gain awareness of how they use these feelings, what their rules are for using them, and how these feelings affect the communication in and the outcome of the relationship.

Through learning, exploring, and practicing new ways of talking, people can use communication workshops as an opportunity to change their patterns of relating. They can alter the ways they feel about themselves and their relationships with family members and other people.

Virginia Satir invented various nourishing and nonthreatening communication experiences. Though she continued to amplify and expand her repertoire of these experiences and their presentation, her basic philosophy remained constant. So did her commitment to her beliefs that:

◇ Each person is a unique miracle.

◇ Growth and learning are always possible.

◇ People are doing the best they can with what they have at any moment.

◇ All behavior can be seen as an effort to grow and not as a comment on "whether I love you."

FOCUSING ON COMFORT

Concern for each person's physical and emotional comfort takes high priority during any workshop session. People learn best when they are comfortable. Body needs are constant, as are pulls from outside commitments. To help people relax more, check out basic comfort factors and introduce any relevant data immediately.

1. Check out that everyone can see and hear you, that you can hear them, and make any necessary changes.

2. Make sure the temperature is at a comfortable level.

3. Give whatever information is necessary for people to be comfortable with their new surroundings: where the telephones, toilets, water fountains are; whether and where refreshments exist; and so forth.

4. Ask whether anyone has special needs that require special provisions.

5. Give general explanations of what will be happening (to reduce anxiety).

6. Model the freedom to comment and reinforce it by giving everyone the opportunity to comment freely and to question.

Attention to comfort conveys your care, concern, and respect for the dignity of each person. It is ego-enhancing and raises self-esteem.

The way you go about creating an atmosphere of comfort is uniquely yours. Allowing ample time for this part is important. People's needs change, so it is important to begin each time you meet by paying attention to these "housekeeping details." Believing that one mention takes care of all details is unrealistic, so be prepared to go through the details as often as necessary.

We cannot emphasize too strongly that by attending carefully to the comfort of each person, you demonstrate that creating an arena for congruency depends on helping people feel comfortable. This means continually giving, receiving, and checking out any information necessary for everyone, including yourself, to become as physically and emotionally comfortable as possible.

FOCUSING
ON CONTACT

Next in importance is to help people feel
connected. Making and maintaining direct contact
with each person is essential. Creating
opportunities for people in the group to connect
directly with each other is likewise critical.
Establishing comfort and contact helps provide
an atmosphere of trust and safety in which
participants have the greatest potential for
learning. Making contact is basic to raising feelings
of self-esteem.

TIMING

"Making haste slowly" is an important rule of
thumb. Processing a few experiences in depth,
slowly and carefully, has greater learning value
than covering too much material once over lightly.

To use time more effectively and efficiently,
we have framed each exercise experience with
a beginning, middle, and end. Each is a complete
entity and can stand alone in demonstrating a
particular concept. However, the beginning of

each exercise is a foundation and needs to be understood before you add any superstructure. Allow sufficient and unhurried time.

The frame is like a page-marker that lets you know where you are in relation to the whole. Since the experiences have the potential for leading into other areas spontaneously, you may be tempted to let that happen. This is not necessarily a good or bad idea, and you can discuss and decide with the group whether to go on with the "happening," postpone it, or proceed with the exercise.

Even with the most careful planning, you may not always complete a whole experience. Acknowledging this as a human clock dilemma is itself a closure and is preferable to racing against time merely to reach the finish.

BEGINNINGS

Waiting for everyone to arrive before beginning a session may be lengthy. For whatever reason, some will arrive later than the specified time. Those who are present may be uncomfortable due not only to the delay but also the strangeness and newness of the situation. For a first session, waiting seems to maximize the use of time (rather than repeatedly stopping and integrating latecomers into the group). It's important to comment on the situation so that the group is aware of your decision to wait.

In later sessions, beginning on time is appropriate and does not penalize those who are there and ready. It's also necessary to acknowledge people who come in late and to integrate them into the group. (Portions of some exercises describe what is involved in entering or leaving ongoing situations.)

ASKING FOR PARTICIPATION

This communication workshop is experiential. Conducting exercises means asking people to participate much of the time. The fact that people are present is no reason to assume that they have already agreed to participate rather than observe. Asking for consent when introducing someone to a new experience is a matter of courtesy and respect. This is also true when asking someone to volunteer to help you demonstrate a point. At times, you may hear a "no." Acknowledging a "no" underscores any person's right to do what fits him or her at that moment.

People have various feelings about going into
something new. Be aware of this when you ask
for participation. Check out how people feel
about their agreement to go into a new experience.
Although this does not automatically eliminate
uncomfortable feelings, your sensitivity to and
acknowledgement of their feelings can help them
become willing to participate more fully.

ASKING ABOUT EXPECTATIONS

Everyone comes into a situation with a picture.
Every picture is colored by invisible veils of
expectations. It is important to give each person
an opportunity to say what he or she wishes and
hopes for, no matter how fantastic or improbable.

How you manage this depends on the size of
the group and the time available. You may ask
the entire group or divide them into smaller
groupings. In the latter case, someone from each
grouping reports back when the entire group
reconvenes so that all hopes and expectations are
shared. Writing them on a flip chart is advisable.

Achieving clarity with the group about their hopes,
wishes, and expectations is a part of learning
about overt, clear, and straight communication.

The potential trap here is that having things straight can be confused with the idea that everyone's wishes and expectations will be fulfilled.

There are differences between what people hope will happen, your plans and ideas, and the realities of what will actually occur. Making this clear is vital to gaining trust. You may want to comment on a prevalent attitude that expectations are labeled "bad" if they don't come about and "good" if they do. Suggesting that we may view differences in expectations as simply "different" may be a new and refreshing alternative. Disappointment and pain are still possible when one's expectations are not met, but such an explanation can help people understand these responses.

BUILDING BRIDGES

Whether at the start of your program, after breaks for coffee or lunch, or after intervals of a day or weeks, it's advisable to *build bridges*. This means acknowledging and responding when people are in the process of moving from where they were to where they are, from what they have been doing to what may be coming next. These transitions can create feelings of unease. By giving information that connects one situation, place, time, or activity to another, you again help make your participants more comfortable. It's similar to having a good road map while exploring new territories.

At the beginning of a second session, for example, you might say, "Time has passed since our last meeting, many things have happened, so let's take a moment to think of how we each have made those necessary steps to move back here. What did you have to do to make this possible?

"In everyday life, we may move from place to place automatically, without acknowledging the need to shift gears. How does that feel? How does that affect how we enter the next project or how we leave our last project?"

Or, "When we last were together, we were speaking of..... Let's find out how you want to proceed into this next part."

UNDERSCORING ENDINGS

When people have been together for a time and will be separating, ask them to say good-bye to each other in some manner. Marking endings in a definitive way makes us much more aware of our many feelings about and reactions to any kind of a separation. These are normal and frequent. Even in one day, people move from the end of one activity to another, or from being in one kind of a relationship to another. When resultant feelings and reactions are outside our awareness, they significantly affect our way of communicating and interacting.

Although people can remain in the same groups for several exercises, it makes for more interest to vary the length of time, the size, and the make-up of the groupings. Regrouping is also a way for everyone in the group to connect with other participants. Through repetitively underscoring endings and making them obvious, you give people opportunities to increase awareness of their feelings, see them as natural and appropriate to endings, and sharpen their skills for handling them.

Another part of endings is that people may be entering into something new and the unknown. This can be a rich source of feelings and reactions which also affect the way we handle our communication at that specific time.

Endings are also inherently and inevitably accompanied by change. Change is another arena of our daily lives that occurs with regularity and stimulates feelings and reactions about which we may be partially or totally unaware. Its effect on communication can sometimes be critical or traumatic.

People can discuss all the above concerning endings and changes during any general discussion period whenever the subject comes up. Such discussions are a valuable part of learning. Endings can be equally useful as a time to take care of any unresolved issues or questions and permit a smoother flow into the next step of your workshop.

LISTENING AND RESPONDING

It is essential to listen and respond to participants' statements with focused attention. Your task is not to judge or interpret what is said but to explore and clarify the what and the how of what is said:

◇ What was actually and literally said; what words were used, what expressions were manifested

◇ How clearly, directly, and specifically it was said

◇ What you heard

◇ What kind of nonverbal messages you
   observed and want to check out for
   meaning

◇ Any difference between what was said
   and what was heard

USING FEEDBACK

Feedback is the information you ask for and
receive about an experience. This barometer can
indicate how the workshop is meeting the
members' needs and expectations. At times, you
may find it desirable to alter, postpone, or adjust
the material you are presenting. It's helpful to
be flexible in terms of making creative adaptations
in your format. However, if you believe a
particular change would seriously impair your
effectiveness, you certainly can state your position.

Before coming to any decision about changing,
ask for everyone's perceptions. Again, you will be
a model, this time for demonstrating a reasonable,
nonadversarial way to make decisions. This means
giving every person the chance to state his or
her feelings, thoughts, ideas, and realities rather
than declaring, "You must do it my way because
I'm in charge and I have the power!" Your job
is to guide the process, not push it.

TAKING BREAKS

Having a break every hour or so is important.
How you manage the break will depend on the
facilities available and the people in the group.
You can plan anything from a stretch or coffee
break to a more elaborate interval with
arrangements for sports or other activities. Discuss
this beforehand with the organizer or sponsor.

RECAPPING

A communication workshop has many important
messages to offer. Ending a session before
adjourning for a day, several days, or weeks
requires a succinct statement about the thread
and the meaning of that particular session.
Defining the learnings of the day is valuable for
you as well as for the group: it provides a sense of
clarity and focus that helps remind everyone
what was important and of use. It also guards
against fragmentation.

Format Suggestions

This chapter presents pictures for planning workshops of varying lengths of time. Every workshop shares basic elements, and an ongoing series permits the inclusion of additional exercises that offer deeper experiences.

DESIGNING A FIRST OR ONLY SESSION

Putting people at ease is important during a first encounter. Again, we offer these ideas to help stimulate your own thinking and planning.

◇ Have quiet, meditative music playing as people gather.

◇ Introduce the organizer and facilitators.

◇ Discuss housekeeping details.

Make contact with the people in the group in whatever way possible, and find ways for them to make some contact with each other.

◇ Listen to and write down the participants' expectations.

◇ Make a "contract" with the group as to what is possible and what is hoped for.

Give a centering exercise, appropriate to the group. (If this is a group that has had little or no experience in workshops of this nature, be especially sensitive as to what you suggest.)

Set the context: briefly explain the ideas behind the communication workshop or series.

Suggest that people keep journals.

Acknowledge that this will be a new experience, invite people's participation, and validate their risk-taking.

Describe and present the first group of exercises involving an awareness of the physical factors that affect communication. Starting with "Temperature Taking" (see chapter 5) is a possibility, especially the sections about what information is needed, and about people's concerns, worries, or wishes.

It's productive to use a flip chart. Write the title "What Affects Communication" and start a list of factors as you present the exercises. (The first two would be *comfort* and *body position*. See Appendix 1 for a comprehensive list.)

At the end of the day, ask for feedback as to what this day was like. You could recommend some home practice if it would fit for the group. Make a wrap-up statement before the closure. The closure can be a simple meditation that bridges this session with another. If this is a single workshop, it serves as the ending. In either event, acknowledge any learning that has occurred, people's willingness to cope (separately from the group) with any unfinished business, and their freedom to leave behind what has not been useful.

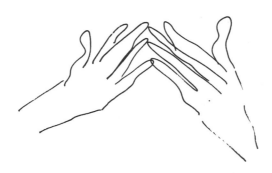

DESIGNING
INTERMEDIATE SESSIONS

It's essential to appreciate that time has passed since the last workshop, whether it be a day, a week, or longer. To help participants feel at ease in the present session, make a bridge from the past one. Also, some people may be absent and some new people may be present, so make any necessary introductions.

Here is a skeletal format to help you plan.

◇ Music as people gather

◇ Bridging remarks

◇ "Temperature Taking"

◇ Centering by guided imagery, limbering exercises, moving to music, or cross-crawl exercises*

◇ Experiences that fit the group's needs

◇ A Satir videotape with discussion and feedback

---

*See John Thie et al., *Touch For Health*. Marina del Rey, CA: De Vorss & Co., 1979.

◊ Suggestions for a practice session at home

◊ Recap

◊ Closure with soft background music and
   a meditation to bridge the current session
   with the following one

DESIGNING A
FINAL SESSION

The workshop's final session helps consolidate
people's sense of exploration and change. It can
also be full of important information for you,
the facilitator(s).

Given your particular group and context, you
can embellish this basic format:

◊ Music as people gather

◊ Bridging remarks

◊ Meditation or centering

◊ "Temperature Taking"

◊ Exercises

Ask for feedback from the group as to the entire experience. Have participants group themselves in triads and report back about:

◇ What people learned

◇ How they feel about the experience

◇ What they may find useful from this workshop

◇ What was missing for people and any recommendations they have

◇ How they believe they can use their learnings

Process the feedback with the entire group. Help people compare what has happened in relation to their original expectations.

◇ Recap

◇ Closure (Acknowledge the learning and risk-taking, and affirm that every participant can choose to take what fits and leave what doesn't.)

◇ Asking that everyone find some way of saying good-bye

Administrative details for the last session are
covered in chapter 1. You may want to prepare
a checklist to remember things like mailing lists,
follow-up forms, and the like.

Part II.
Exercises and
Experiences

The suggestions in this manual are only examples: they are not carved in marble. Although we present exercises in a certain progression, you can use them in whatever order fits your program. Our suggestions are not meant to stifle your creativity and spontaneity.

What Affects Communication?

◇ Body Position

◇ Reactions

◇ Certain Words and Phrases

◇ Projections, Stereotypes, Rules, and Rumors

◇ Being One of a Triad

◇ Harmonious Triads

◇ Stress

BODY POSITION

Purpose   This group of experiences explores what happens to people as they talk to each other in different physical positions. Thoughts, feelings, body reactions, and behavior resulting from different physical positions affect both the communication and the relationship.

For many, this is a first conscious, deliberate action to focus specifically on one's body responses, feelings, and thoughts. The experience is at once graphic, nonthreatening, and fun, and it can make further exploration more readily acceptable.

Note   *This group of experiences has a number of parts. Depending on the group's makeup and the time available, you may decide to omit certain parts entirely.*

Time   One to two or more hours, depending on the total number of parts covered, the number of people in the group, and the pacing of your program.

Description   Ask each person to look around
                         the room carefully and think
Part 1   about someone in the group he
                         or she would like to be with.
After a few minutes, ask everyone to get up and,
without talking, choose a partner. Have them
sit comfortably, with enough space around them
so that conversations between couples won't
intrude on one another.

After the couples are seated, ask for their attention
and explain that each couple is to start a
conversation about a topic you suggest—for
instance, "What was it like to choose a partner?"
or "Are you more comfortable choosing someone
you know or a stranger?" or "What is real in your
life for you now?" They are to face each other
and talk while maintaining direct eye contact.
They may find themselves looking away from
each other from time to time; ask them to be
aware of that.

Explain that you will interrupt from time to time
to give other instructions. To give support, you
may also want to indicate that all of this could feel
somewhat awkward and strange at first. It is
natural for people to have such feelings when
attempting anything new.

After ten or fifteen minutes, or whenever everyone
appears to be talking freely, interrupt. You may
begin a general discussion about this experience or
wait until after the next part.

Part 2   Ask that everyone turn his or her chair completely around so that each person sits back to back, with at least six inches between the chairs (to ensure that the chairs are not touching). The couples continue their conversations in this position.

After five minutes or so, interrupt. Announce the interruption with, "I am now interrupting you." This statement helps people become conscious of the many interruptions in daily living, and how they usually don't recognize their accompanying feelings, how they handle those feelings, and how their communication is therefore affected.

Begin a discussion about what the experience has been like up to this point. As people make comments, add questions that call attention to thoughts, reactions, and feelings they had and conclusions and assumptions that they made. Here are some examples:

> "What differences were you aware of in your body when you faced each other as opposed to being back to back?"

> "How did each position make you feel about yourself, your partner, and the subject about which you were talking?"

> "When you were back to back, what adjustments did you make to be able to

hear? What effect did that have on
the content of your conversation?
How did that make you feel about
yourself and your partner?"

"How did the change in body position
make you feel? Where did you feel
it in your body? What kind of a
reaction was it?"

"When you were back to back, what
did you notice about your interest
in your partner as compared to your
interest in the other people and things
around you?"

Their answers can be an opportunity for you to
encourage people to acknowledge, amplify, and
clarify their feelings and reactions. Interpreting
or judging is not appropriate.

Take a leisurely pace for the first discussion so
that everyone has ample opportunity to report his
or her experiences. It is important that each one
who wants to speak gets that opportunity,
regardless of time. This demonstrates that
everyone counts, everyone is important, and
everyone's ideas count. If you notice that someone
has not commented, try to direct some remark
that invites a response. (It's not practical to include
everyone in every discussion period, but setting
the tone is crucial in this initial phase.)

People occasionally start discussing experiences
with each other rather than with the entire group.
When that happens, resume the general discussion
by stating that you are interrupting because only
one voice can be heard at a time and you want
everyone to be able to hear and be heard. This
emphasizes the importance of each participant
as well as of the entire group.

Part 3   One partner stands up (or stands
on a chair) and the other sits on the
floor, close to the feet of the first. Partners
maintain eye contact while they continue with
their conversations. After a few minutes, ask that
they reverse positions and continue talking.

After several more minutes, interrupt for a
discussion of what this part was like: what people
were aware of while having this particular
experience. Some may report feelings of being
childlike; others, how easy it was to feel critical
and powerful while standing over someone; or
how natural it was to point down at the person
below with an outstretched, accusing finger.

Part 4   Partners stand up and face each other.
Each person looks over the other's
left shoulder while carrying on the conversation.
This is the "cocktail party syndrome."

During the next discussion, you might inquire
whether people felt more interested in what was
going on around them rather than their partner
and the conversation.

Part 5   Both partners remain standing, facing each other. The first person looks over the head of the other, making no eye contact. The other looks directly at the first partner. After several minutes of conversation, request that they reverse positions.

Part 6   Partners continue to stand and face each other, but they stand at least twelve feet apart as they talk.

As you shout over the noise level, you might inquire if this is a condition with which anyone in the group is familiar? Is it like carrying on a conversation at home, from the kitchen to the living room? Is it possible to really hear anything clearly? What might be the result if the conversations concerned whether the taxes or mortgage had been paid?

Part 7   Each couple comes back together and sits face to face. This time, partners converse while holding a piece of paper or a pillow between them so they cannot make eye contact.

Part 8   Using a mirror large enough to see a person's entire face, the first partner looks at him or herself while talking to the other person. The second partner looks at the first one directly, not in the mirror. After a few minutes, ask that they reverse roles and then discuss with each other what this experience was like.

Part 9   Partners sit comfortably, facing each
other, making eye contact, and holding
hands if they wish. After sitting quietly for a
moment, they are to share what it has been like
to spend this time together.

When people have had an adequate chance to
exchange their experiences, ask that they say
good-bye in whatever way expresses how they
are now feeling about each other.

Group   After completing what you have
Discussion   determined is the final part
of this exercise, reconvene the
entire group for a general discussion about the
experience as a whole. Even though you may
have had discussion periods during or after each
part, it is important to have the total group
together at the end. This engenders a sense of
completion.

During the discussion, underscore the *awarenesses*
that people reported as they changed their body
positions. Questions that could encourage
comments are:

> "What happened to the quality of
> the dialogue as you were in the
> different positions?"

> "What price did you pay in terms
> of physical discomfort to hear the
> other?"

"What were the differing feelings
and thoughts each of you had about
yourself during the different parts
of the exercise?"

"What were the feelings and thoughts
that one person had that you
discovered to have been shared by
the other?"

"What were the ways you handled
feelings that were similar to others in
the group? That were different?"

"What similarities were you aware
of between the exercises and your daily
living activities? What can you learn
from these exercises in terms of
handling those situations more
effectively?"

At some time during the discussion, it's helpful
to observe that we can't always be in the most
perfect position for clear, direct communication.
Just knowing how body positions can affect
communication is significant: difficulties can arise
simply as a result of the physical position rather
than due to someone's perversity or lack of caring,
love, or regard. In other words, if my back is
to you, I can be aware that misunderstandings

may develop because I'm not hearing you well—
rather than concluding that if you love me, you'd
know what I said and if you really loved me,
you'd also know what I meant.

One practical suggestion is that before discussing
a vital matter and exchanging important facts
which also might involve intense feelings, it is best
to begin with everyone in the position most
conducive for giving clear, direct, specific
messages. This means:

> Each person is physically comfortable.

> Outside distractions are minimized
> or postponed.

> Everyone has agreed to have this
> discussion at this time.

> People are at eye level with each other
> and at easy seeing and hearing distance.

These conditions do not guarantee a tranquil
exchange of words and ideas. How people feel
about themselves and the others also makes a
difference. We all have a better chance of being
productive and creative, though, if we begin
with these basics.

Flip Chart   Under "What Affects
Communication," write:

Body position
Comfort level
Interruptions
Connecting with others
The level of your self-esteem

REACTIONS

Purpose   This exercise shows that ordinary
events such as interruptions,
decision-making, and planning often produce
stress and tension. They affect communication,
which in turn affects our feelings, thoughts,
behavior and, ultimately, our relationships.

It is possible to discriminate between a situation
and what arises out of a situation. This distinction
cannot eliminate the feelings that we have, but
it can alter the ways we handle them so that:

> Differences of opinion can contribute
> to the creative growth of a relationship
> rather that producing conflict.

> Decision-making can become a matter
> of reality, not simply an indication
> of who has the power or who is the
> boss.

> Choices can provide the risk and the
> adventure that lead to new experiences
> and renew relationships.

> Changes and interruptions can be
> an opportunity to move in another

direction or can create relief and a
change of pace.

This exercise's format and manner of presentation
also demonstrate that it is possible to create an
atmosphere in which we focus on the *how* and
what of an experience, rather than evaluating
its content. Simultaneously, it sharpens our
awareness of how we unknowingly impose value
judgments and rules on certain feelings. We also
recognize how these rules and values are filters
through which our communication travels and
becomes contaminated.

This experience dramatizes that whatever feelings
result from stress, they are natural and normal
reactions. It helps to realize that every other person
present shares many of these feelings.

Time   The total time for this exercise group
             can be from one hour to two hours
or more. Allow sufficient time during the different
parts of this exercise so participants make enough
of a connection with their groups. This is needed if
they are to experience real feelings about the
changes and separations during this exercise.

Description   Ask each person to think of
                    a partner, allowing time to
Part 1   select someone deliberately
                    (perhaps basing the decision
on a definite reason). After thinking for a few

minutes, each person silently gets up, goes to
the chosen person, sits down directly in front of
him or her, and waits silently for further
instructions. You may want to explain that the
reason for silence is to stay in touch with one's
feelings during these moments of change.

Part 2   When all couples are seated, ask that
                 they close their eyes. Have them
reflect silently while you ask some of the following
questions.

> "What was it like to be in the position
> of having to make a choice?"

> "Did you base your decision on
> whether to go to someone or to wait
> and see who would come to you?"

> "What was it like to find that the person
> you wanted had already been chosen
> by someone else, if that happened
> to you?"

You can shorten or lengthen this part, depending
on the group's sophistication. Five or ten seconds
may be long enough for people who are new
to this kind of experience.

Ask people to open their eyes and begin a
conversation with their partners. They may want
to share what this experience was like and how
it differed from the previous one.

After ten or fifteen minutes, interrupt and ask that people again close their eyes. Invite them to be aware of what they felt as they were interrupted.

Then ask that they open their eyes while you explain the next part.

Part 3 Each couple discusses and decides which other couple they would like to join (to make units of four people). Set a limit of about ten or fifteen minutes for the decision-making. You may want to announce a three-minute warning before the actual time has elapsed. At the end of the allotted time, give some signal for talking to cease and for people to get up and indicate their selections.

During the shift, you can expect much laughter and confusion until everyone finally settles in their new groups. With that done, ask that they all close their eyes for a moment to center themselves. Then begin a general discussion as to what it was like to create a new group and how that relates to real-life situations.

In addition to the responses from the group, consider suggesting the following:

> "What was it like to go through the decision-making process?"

> "How did you decide whether to choose or be chosen?"

"What was it like to leave an ongoing, familiar situation?"

"What was it like to sit and wait?"

"What was it like to have new people join your twosome?"

"What changes did you notice when moving from one place to another, from one group to another?"

"What was it like to come into an ongoing situation, where two people had a relationship with each other before your arrival?"

"What was it like to find the couple you chose had already been chosen, if that was what happened? How did each couple cope?"

"What adjustments were necessary just because there was an increase in the number of people in the group?"

Part 4   Within each group, have people share their experiences of going from two people to four and how this relates to their own lives. Allow fifteen minutes or more.

If time is a factor, this can be an appropriate place to end; if so, you may want to extend the discussion to thirty minutes.

Part 5 Each group decides which member of the group will leave the group and join another. The departing person then thinks of a group he or she would like to join. Give the groups fifteen minutes or so to decide. Then signal so all departees start at the same time to go and sit with a new group.

Discussion After at least twenty minutes for the new groups to make new connections, have a general discussion as to people's experiences during this part of the exercise:

> "When you make an internal decision, how do you feel about stating your preference to others? How do you feel when others state their preferences?"

> "What went into your own private decision about whether to leave or stay? Did that differ from what you expressed to your group?"

> "In your daily life, how do you approach and handle making decisions?"

> "What happened internally when you had to wait longer for your turn to

talk, because now there were four people to divide time and space instead of two?"

"What was it like to want to interrupt? What skills and rules do you have and use for interrupting? What kinds of feelings occur when you interrupt others or when you are interrupted?"

When the discussion winds down, ask that each group bid its members good-bye in a way that expresses their feelings.

Flip Chart   Under "What Affects Communication," add:

Making decisions

Planning

Changing the numbers of a group

Leaving an ongoing situation

Entering a new situation

Having one's choices accepted

Having one's choices not accepted

Being disappointed

Having rules about how to handle situations

Being included

Being excluded

CERTAIN WORDS
AND PHRASES

Purpose   This exercise brings to people's awareness how using direct, personal pronouns and certain other words can alter what they say and respond to.

Time   Thirty minutes

Description   People experiment in couples, using only certain phrases as they talk. After each person has had a turn, the pairs discuss what the experience felt like.

Part 1   After people have chosen partners, they sit and face each other. One person chooses the letter A; the other, B.
A begins a short discussion of three or four sentences of something of interest to him or her at this time.

B responds, using only the following phrases to begin each statement, one after the other. A is not to answer B but to concentrate on his or her feelings as B makes each of these responses.

"It is obvious to me that ..."

"I imagine you felt ..."

"It is my guess that ..."

"I am ..."

"I imagine you disliked ..."

"I should ..."

After each person has had a turn, ask that the dyads spend a few minutes talking about what this was like.

Part 2   Ask the couples to continue their conversations without the above restrictions. Instead, each is to talk or ask questions that always begin with the pronoun "it." After a few minutes, ask them to switch to the pronoun "you." After another few minutes, ask that they now begin only with the pronoun "I."

Discussion   The group reconvenes for a general discussion, sharing what happened and how people felt about themselves and their partners as they used the different pronouns.

Flip Chart   Under "What Affects Communication," add:

Use of certain words and phrases

Use of indirect, impersonal pronouns

Use of direct, personal pronouns

PROJECTIONS, STEREOTYPES, RULES, AND RUMORS*

Purpose   This experience demonstrates how preconceptions, prejudices, and assumptions influence a relationship. We act on our perceptions, but our perceptions of the present often mix with images from the past. Knowledge alone is not enough to change these perceptions. This exercise permits people to recognize and experience those internal messages and rules that preclude, distort, or curtail the growth of close, meaningful relationships. It also indicates how to begin transcending those influences.

Time   This exercise requires one and a half to two hours. It is best done after people have completed other exercises together and have feelings of community, safety, and trust. You may want to break before the group discussion or to complete the experience with only a stretch break.

---

*Also called "With Whom Am I Having the Pleasure?" These words were transcribed from Virginia Satir by Michele Baldwin and Ken Block of the Avanta Network, at Process Community III in August 1983. This was one of the many times Virginia has presented this exercise.

Description   While partners sit facing each other, you present a series of comments. Participants respond silently, within themselves. Speak slowly and distinctly as you present the exercise and allow time for people to absorb the words and to be in touch with any internal responses. Make any necessary arrangements to ensure that there are no distractions or intrusions. After the exercise, reconvene the group for a general discussion.

The following are Virginia Satir's words. You may choose to use these words or your own.

Part 1   "Look around the room and select someone with

Getting Started   whom you are interested in spending the next half hour to explore new ways of relating and to learn about the process of beginning a relationship. Perhaps you could choose someone whom you do not yet know. When you have privately decided, close your eyes and think about what you are about to do. Notice any body responses. Give yourself permission to act on your selection. Breathe. Now, go find a partner nonverbally."

After the group settles themselves in couples, begin the next part.

"You may have ended up with the person you selected. You may not have been so fortunate. Nevertheless, all of you have been 100 percent successful. Each of you has found a partner. Congratulate yourselves. Sit down in front of each other, knee to knee. Position yourselves for optimum eye contact. Do this without talking.

"Close your eyes and be in touch with your body, your breathing. Notice any tight places. Let yourself relax. Pay exquisite attention to my voice. A relaxed body accompanies an alert mind. With your eyes still closed, be aware that you are, as at the beginning of all new relationships, strangers. You can be sure that you and your partner have a lot in common and many differences, as well.

Part 2

Like a Camera

"With your eyes still closed, think of yourself as a camera. Have the ability, at my direction, to open and close your eyes in a split second, swiftly, like the shutter in the lens of a camera. Take a picture and develop it in your own mind now. Look at the picture that you just took.

What are you thinking?

What are you feeling?

What is happening in your body?

"Again, allow yourself to notice your breathing and any tension that may have developed in your body. Allow yourself to relax.

Part 3   "Open your eyes now and
                     look at the person in front of
Projections   you. Never mind what your
("Hanging Hats")   mother said, looking isn't
                     staring. It's OK. Look for any
evidence of whom this person may remind you
of: people in your present or past, celebrities,
historical figures, literary characters, etc. Whether
it is a little reminder or a big one, let it enter into
your awareness.

"Look carefully, and when you have someone
in mind, alternate it with the picture of the person
across form you. Notice any changes that may
occur in your body, any changes in your breathing.
Ask yourself:

What do you think about that person?

How do you feel as you become aware
of your thoughts?

What are you aware of in your body?

Part 4   "Open your eyes.
                            Notice what stands
Stereotypes   out for you most
("What Stands Out for You?") about the person
                            that you are sitting
with. It could be age, sex, color, hair style, teeth
arrangement. It could be almost anything.

"Become aware of any prejudices that are activated in you by what you noticed, be they positive or negative. Now, close your eyes and again ask yourself:

What are you thinking?

What are you feeling?

What are your body reactions?

"Does the information [of which you have become aware] to this point lengthen or shorten the bridge between you and your partner? What do you know now that you did not know when you first sat down?

"With your eyes still closed, ask yourself what you think the person across form you is thinking and feeling about you. Allow yourself to fantasize about this, no matter how rich or how unpleasant these thoughts may be. Become aware of how you feel as you tell yourself what you think your partner thinks and feels about you in this moment. Again notice your breathing and any tight places that may have developed in your body during these last minutes of your life. Relax, and alertness will increase.

Part 5

Third-Party Information
("Gossip and Rumor")

"With your eyes still closed, think about any third-party information that you may have about the person with whom you are sharing this time. Where did you acquire this information? How was it presented? What was the intent of the offering? Notice any thoughts, feelings, or bodily reactions that may occur inside you as you become aware of the gossip in your head. With your eyes still closed, ask yourself if you have had any prior experience with this person yourself. Remember in full the nature of that transaction or transactions. What did you tell yourself about that person when you left his or her presence? What did you learn? Again:

What are you thinking?

What are you feeling?

Can you be in touch with any changes in your body?

"Breathe. Relax."

Part 6

Rules About Commenting

"With your eyes still closed, become aware that your head is stuffed with all kinds of data. For the last fifteen minutes or so, you have been generating new information at terrifically skillful speeds. Notice that this information is all of your own making. It has nothing to do with anyone else. You have created it all yourself. If the contact you made with the person across from you were to terminate now, suddenly, all you would be left with are the thoughts and feelings you have generated over the course of this exercise. Be with that for a moment.

"Now, give yourself private permission to share with your partner:

⋄ What you saw, your camera *picture*

⋄ What or who that person reminded you of, your *projection*

⋄ What stood out for you, your *stereotype*

⋄ What *thoughts and feelings* you conjured up that your partner may have thought and felt about you

⋄ What *third-party information* you have about your partner, your gossip; what occurs to you now about your past experiences (if any) with him or her

"Ask yourself what you are thinking and feeling, in this moment, about doing what most people do not do. How do you feel about having given yourself permission to share with your partner your private fantasies about them? You may become aware that you have the thought that goes something like this: 'Oh, I couldn't tell them that! I'd hurt their feelings or embarrass myself.'

"If anything like this is going on with you, notice it, relax, and try to allow yourself to share it anyway.

"Let your eyes gently open, and share now with your partner what this has been like for you."

Allow 30 to 45 minutes for this discussion.

"I am now interrupting you. I am a voice coming in. You may have felt jarred. Be aware that this is not my intent.

"Close your eyes once more and become aware of how you are feeling in this moment. What are you thinking? How is your body responding? If you were to take a picture now, how would it differ from the first? If you notice no difference, ask yourself, 'How come?'

"So, now take that picture and look at it. Open your eyes and close them, like the shutter on the camera. Is the picture different? How?

Processing in the Larger Group

"With your eyes now open:

"How many of you saw a different picture at the end than at the beginning?

"How many of you found that your partner reminded you of someone else?

"IIow many of you noticed something that stood out for you about your partner?

"How many of you had thoughts or feelings in your mind or guts, born of past experience?

"How many of you dealt with your inside information differently than in past experiences of meeting someone new?

"Would a couple come forward and be willing to share your experience with the large group?"

Discussion

At this time, either a couple comes up to share their experiences, or you can ask for comments from the group as a whole.

Flip Chart   Under "What Affects
                        Communication," add:

                        Projections

                        Preconceptions

                        Stereotypes

                        Prejudices

                        Rumors

BEING ONE OF A TRIAD

Purpose   This exercise illustrates the physical difficulties encountered when three people rather than two are having a discussion. Adjustments are necessary to have a meaningful sharing and still use the support, energies, and resources of all three persons. The "observer" may feel left out or uninvolved, especially when he or she is not actively participating. It can then also appear that the observer has no impact on and is not giving any energy to the triad.

This exercise shows that the observer is indeed a part of what happens in a triad. However, it is natural for the observer to struggle for inclusion when two others are involved with each other. Despite knowing that exclusion is not their intent, the third person may still feel left out, abandoned, or helpless.

How do people handle those feelings? What are their options? How do their feelings affect behavior?

Verbally and nonverbally, this experience shows that nourishment, creativity, cooperation, and trust can be a reality within a triad. Participants can transcend the generally accepted belief that having three people together makes for trouble because it necessarily becomes two against one.

Time   About one hour

Description   In groups of three, participants experience how it is to be an observer at certain times and an active participant at others.

We have indicated discussion periods to be carried on with each triad, following each part of the exercise. You may want to defer these until after several parts or the entire exercise. Also, you can hold a group discussion after the different parts or at completion.

Part 1   Ask people to arrange themselves in groups of three, make themselves comfortable, and sit so that all three can easily see and hear each other. Each person selects a letter: A, B, or C.

Ask that people close their eyes for a few seconds, then open their eyes and stand up, forming a triangle, facing straight ahead, not looking at each other.

Next, have them move so that they can see each other. B and C begin a discussion, turning to face each other. A only observes, without entering the discussion.

After a few minutes, interrupt and ask that they rotate roles so each person has the opportunity to observe.

Part 2   This time B and C look at each other
while A tries to interrupt nonverbally.
After a short time, rotate this exercise so each
person is in the position of interrupting. After each
person has had a turn, ask that people stop, sit
down, close their eyes, and be aware of what they
are feeling. How is each one feeling about the
other members of their triad?

After a few seconds, have them open their eyes
and share with their triad what this part was like.

Part 3   For the next part, B and C stand side
by side and turn their backs to A.
After a minute or so of this silent tableau, have
them rotate roles. Finally, have all three people
share what this was like.

Part 4   Next, B and C vie nonverbally,
perhaps even physically, for the
attention of A. Again, ask at intervals that they
rotate positions so each experiences being vied for.

Part 5   Ask that each group sit in a triangle
and that people close their eyes. They
are to imagine an open basket in the center of
the triad at knee level. With their eyes still closed,
they put their own hands together in the form
of a V—palms touching and fingertips apart—just
at the navel. Using a rhythmic motion, each person
makes symbolical gestures of putting their
resources into the imaginary basket. From this
imaginary basket, each person also symbolically
takes out the resources he or she needs.

As this is happening, ask participants to be aware of the rhythm of their movements, of making contact with another's hands, or of making no contact.

After several minutes, they open their eyes and ready themselves for the next part.

Part 6   Ask people to get comfortable, close their eyes, and be in touch with how their bodies are feeling. Then have them look at each other in silence, honoring each other and themselves, and becoming aware that being in a triad always offers three possibilities:

To be with oneself

To be with one other

To be together as three

Any triad has these potential combinations: A, B, C are three units of one; A—B, A—C, and B—C make three pairing units; and A—B—C makes one triad. These represent the sources of energy in any triad.

To illustrate this nonverbally, ask everyone to stand. First, each person gets in touch with him- or herself. Have people embrace themselves by wrapping their own arms around themselves. Next, have them make a physical connection with other, in pairs, in their own fashion. Finally, ask all three to connect physically as a triad.

Part 7   Have participants move away from their triads, to be on their own, not touching another. Then, ask them to become aware that this gesture of separating is not a comment on anyone's love, that it perhaps may come as a relief. Moving away is a statement that represents "what fits for me, now, here at this place."

Last, have them say good-bye to each member in whatever way they choose to acknowledge their feelings about living for a time as a triad.

Discussion   If you like, this is a time to begin a general discussion of the entire experience.

Flip Chart   Under "What Affects Communication," add:

Being one of three

Feeling left out

Feeling discriminated against

Feeling ignored

Feeling excluded

Feeling abandoned

Feeling included

Trying to break into an ongoing situation

Feeling responsible for the comfort of an observer

HARMONIOUS TRIADS

Purpose This experience offers a way to form a harmonious triad with two other people. It explores the kinds of connections that are possible when three people are together and how communication differs. Having three people also affects what is necessary to reach decisions and how the process becomes more complex and involved.

Part of the exercise entails an experience that is common to daily life: moving from one group or situation to another. How do people cope with and integrate the leaving and entering, which can entail feelings of being disoriented, out of balance, and uprooted? The purpose here is to handle fears of being rejected yet allow feelings of joy and anticipation.

Time Two hours

Description People form into triads and spend fifteen minutes talking together. They then take five minutes to decide which one member will leave to join another triad.

The newly formed triads spend fifteen minutes together, then another five minutes to decide

again which member will leave. This repeats
until there have been three changes in all. After
the third change, people rejoin their original triads.
A general discussion follows.

Part 1   Each participant thinks of two other
persons he or she would like to be
with and joins together into a triad. Members
each choose a letter: A, B, or C. Still standing,
they make themselves comfortable in their triad
and arrange themselves so as to be able to see
each other easily.

Ask that each A turn around slowly so that B
and C can see all sides of A. Then B and C report
what they actually saw as A turned. B and C
will then take turns and do the same. The reports
should include:

◇ What the observers see about the person
   who turns: physical details, clothes, facial
   expressions, and so on

◇ What it was like for the observers to watch
   the person who was turning

◇ Anything about the turning person that
   reminded the observers of someone else

After the observers report, the third person shares
what he or she felt while turning and being
observed by two other people.

Part 2   Ask the triads to sit down and discuss for fifteen minutes what is of most importance in each person's life at the present. Then have them spend five minutes to decide which member of the triad is to leave and join another. After calling time, ask that those members join another group and form a new triad.

Part 3   The newly formed triads repeat the same process as in Parts 1 and 2. This repeats once more, making a total of three times. After the third time, people rejoin their original triads.

Part 4   When people return to their original triads, supply everyone with paper and pencil. Each person lists the experiences he or she had during the entire exercise and then reads the list to the other two. As they listen, people add the experiences of the two other members to their own lists. At the finish, each triad member has a list of all the experiences of all three members.

Part 5   Have the entire group reconvene for a general discussion. A representative from each triad reads the list of their experiences. You may want to write these items on a flip chart so everyone can see the similarities and differences of how people handled their experiences and feelings during this exercise.

Simultaneously, each person adds any new experiences and feelings to his or her own list,

so that everybody ends up with a total listing
of each other's experiences during this exercise.

Flip Chart   Under "What Affects
Communication," add:

Being conscious of being carefully
observed from all angles by two
others

Being in a new group of people

Having to incorporate a new
person into an existing dyad

Leaving familiar situations

Moving back to one's original
group or "connection"

STRESS

Purpose   What is said, how it is said, and how people react during stressful situations is often outside our awareness. This exercise dramatizes that we usually cope by responding to the stress rather than being in touch with the situation and the people involved. The exercise also presents ways to transform these automatic responses into ones that recognize other available choices.

Having choices for responding becomes an important tool when stress occurs in a relationship. Feeling stress threatens people's intentions and wishes for satisfying relationships, and their reactions are often due more to the stress than to problems in the relationship. The first step, then, is to cope with the stress: each person does whatever is necessary to become comfortable. They can then attend to the difficulty or problem they are having.

Time   Two to three hours. If you have a limited schedule, the first part is of value and can be done in one hour or less.

Description   An important contribution toward understanding the ways people handle and respond to stress in

relationships has been made by Viginia Satir.
She calls this concept *communication stances.*
In her many years of working with people, she
observed that we respond to stress in one of five
fairly predictable ways, or stances, and we
respond not so much to the situation itself as to
the stress.

These stances are best learned visually, through
demonstration, in addition to your words. Ask
for volunteers or use yourself. As another aid, write
the stances on the flip chart.

Here are the stances, their respective body
positions, and the feelings that each represents.

> 1. The placater or martyr. In this stance,
>   a person under stress agrees to whatever
>   is said or suggested, no matter what he
>   or she feels or believes. The only way this
>   person thinks he or she can get along is
>   to allow other people to have their own
>   way. The placater uses words of agreement.
>   The body position is down on one knee
>   with one hand over the heart, the other arm
>   outstretched in a pleading manner.
>
> 2. The blamer, accuser, or attacker. The
>   attitude in this stance is that no matter what
>   happens, it's always the other person's
>   fault. Blamers use words of blame. The
>   body position is to stand with one hand on
>   hip, the other arm extended with the index

finger stiffly pointing straight out; body weight is on the front leg.

3. The super-reasonable one or the computer. In this stance, the person ignores the feelings or needs of everyone, including him- or herself. The situation itself is what is important, and it is handles by rules set down by the Constitution, the Bible, Emily Post, and so on. The super-reasonable one's words are pedantic and refer to authorities, rules, and shoulds. The body position is to hold the head high, to stand completely erect and stiff, with the hands folded together in front in a preaching position, and to look over people, not at them.

4. The distracter or the irrelevant one. The way to handle stress in this stance is to ignore everything completely: oneself, the other person, and the situation. The distracter may be constantly in motion, change the subject, or be physically distracting, escape into drugs, alcohol, or work; or actually leave the scene. The distracter's words do not address the meat of the matter at hand. The body position is one of constant, aimless motion.

5. The congruent responder. In this stance, the person takes into account him- or herself as well as the others involved, the

situation, and the realities. Communication is clear, direct, and specific; the congruent person gives and checks out facts and information. The body position is one of comfort and ease. (Congruence also includes the other four responses *when they are made by choice.*)

Part 1   This exercise involves asking people to experiment with using their bodies differently, as explanations convey less than direct experience. Many ways exist to present the stances; this is only one of them.

After the description and demonstration, ask participants to arrange themselves into groups of five. Ask that each person take a letter: A, B, C, D, or E.

Before starting the exercise, ask for questions to clarify any confusion. Then ask how people are feeling about what they are going to do. (Also, after each part of this experiment, ask what people are aware of and how they are feeling about what they were doing.)

Start with a practice session. Each group starts a conversation in which everyone uses placating responses, with both words and the martyrlike body position. Typical placating response are:

"It's all my fault, dear."

"Whatever you want, dear."

"Don't worry about what I want."

"I just want to please you, dear."

Next, ask that everyone practice the blaming response. Typical examples are:

"Why do you always ...?"

"Why don't you ever ...?"

"You never let me ...."

"It's always your fault that ...."

"If it weren't for you ...."

Next, everyone practices the super-reasonable response. Each person speaks in generalities, cites authorities and sources, and uses impersonal, indirect pronouns with long and complicated words.

For the distracting response, people shift from one subject to another, never answer a question directly, and engage in distracting behavior such as whistling, humming, jumping around, pulling at others, and so forth.

Part 2   Allow people time to get comfortable after practicing these stances. Then have each group start a conversation. Following a format you decide and write on the flip chart, each person responds verbally in the manner of one of the four communication stances.

For instance, at first:

All the A's respond as placaters

All the B's as blamers

All the C's as distracters

All the D's and E's as computers

After several minutes, interrupt and ask participants to change their responses according to another format on the flip chart. Repeat this several times until you observe that everyone has become quite competent at each stance.

Have a general discussion of experiences people had. What were their physical reactions? How did they feel about themselves and others? What happened to the conversations they were having? And in which of these positions did people feel a certain familiarity?

Part 3   Follow the above procedure for assigning and switching responses, but this time have participants respond without words, using body positions only. It's important to have the complete format written on the flip chart so people can refer to it as needed. As people take each position, let them freeze that stance for a minute or so before you ask them to change into the next one. This lets people really comprehend the physical feel of each position.

Part 4   Ask participants to take a stance of their own choosing, hold that position until it feels comfortable, then change to another. Have them continue changing at their own pace. After two or three changes, ask that everyone freeze in whatever position they are in.

Ask for a very brief report from a few people about what they are feeling physically, how comfortable they are in those positions, and what they are aware of about the others in their group.

Explain that each person is now to make *only one* move to be more comfortable. That done, again ask people to make one move toward making themselves comfortable. Continue in this fashion until each person is physically comfortable and is sitting down.

Discussion   Begin a discussion as to what people observed and experienced during the entire exercise.

◊ What differences did they notice in their feelings and bodies in the four stances?

◇ How effectively could they listen to others while in the different positions?

◇ What responses felt familiar? Which were the least familiar? And which were the easiest to enact?

It is important to emphasize that these responses are often automatic, out of awareness, and do not represent our intentions. At other times, however, we use them deliberately: to please someone; when we want our wishes and feedback respected; when we want to use our heads and our intelligence; and when we need a vacation or relief from stress.

You may want to talk again about congruence, the fifth response to stress. People in the congruent stance first make themselves comfortable. Their communication is direct, specific, and clear. They check out assumptions. They distinguish between what they are feeling and the thoughts they express with words. They take into account their own and others' feelings, thoughts, realities, and concerns.

Flip Chart   Under "What Affects Communication," add:

Stress

Create another heading for "Communication Tools" and start a list with:

Sculpting communication stances

Communication
Tools

◇ Mirroring:
   "Do You Mean ...?"

◇ Activating the Ingredients
   of an Interaction

◇ Temperature Taking

◇ Transforming Rules

MIRRORING:
"DO YOU MEAN ...?"

Purpose   Mirroring, the first section of this
                 exercise, offers an experience in
hearing feedback as a request for information
without critical implications. Participants explore
the many ways messages are sent out and received.
They also practice congruent responses.

Any discussion that deteriorates into "Yes, it's
so" and "No, it isn't" becomes a duel of accusation
and defense. Questions come across as blame
or criticism rather than requests for clarification
or information. Sharing ideas is then impossible,
which certainly harms the relationship.

Such scenarios commonly occur when one person's
intended message is either not fully expressed
or not perceived by the listener. Naturally, the
teller is in a better position to know what he or
she intended; the listener knows what he or she
saw and heard. Both people need a way to check
out whether what was said matches what was
meant to be said, and whether what was heard
matches what was meant to be heard. The goal is
not to agree or disagree with what was said, but
to clarify and understand. Only then can a true
meaningful dialogue occur.

The second section of this exercise deals with expanding and extending the meanings of any statement, question, or report. The experience illustrates that every statement or remark has many more meanings than are apparent on the surface.

This exercise is also designed to let people delve into a subject extensively without eliciting defensive reactions of "What did you mean by that?" or "Why did you say that?" The listener instead becomes active in the interchange: he or she introduces questions and ideas that expand the scope of the subject being discussed.

Listeners ask these questions in the context of getting sufficient information to carry on a cogent, rational dialogue. This implies that they feel real interest in what the tellers say. It indicates nonverbally, "I care enough about you to want to know more about what you are saying, and I am putting my energy and effort into our dialogue by participating actively."

Additionally, an important purpose here has to do with the way we ask for information. The exercise distinguishes between "I am stuck because I don't have enough information to ask for the answers I need" and "I don't know because I'm stupid, and I can't ask because then you'll know I'm stupid." People often deprive themselves of necessary facts this way.

The practical applications of this exercise are many. It provides an important and useful tool for checking out information in a nonaggressive, nonthreatening, creative manner. Together with other exercises, it synthesizes the communication process: the giving, receiving, and checking out of information in ways that are clear, direct, and specific. And it provides an ego-enhancing experience.

Note   *Including this exercise is important. It is most effective when your group has developed a sense of community and trust, as many parts can evoke special reactions.*

Time   One and a half to two hours. You can take short breaks after completing the first section and after the different segments of the second section. You may want to hold general discussions at these times.

Description

Part 1   Ask that people form into pairs and pick A or B. A begins by making a short statement of something he or she believes is true. B watches, listens closely, and then tries to mimic A exactly in tone, gestures, words, timing, body position, and expression. (It's helpful to demonstrate this mirroring exercise before people begin.)

A and B then mutually check out whether there
was a match: that what was said matched what
was heard, and what was done with the body
was seen. They continue checking until both agree
that the listener heard exactly what the speaker
said. Then they reverse roles.

Circulate around the room as the group is working,
to help people follow the instructions precisely.
For instance, you may observe and comment that
"It was the third finger on the left hand that
moved upward two inches while he turned his
head down and to the right as he was saying 'It
seems to me'."

After twenty minutes for this part, interrupt and
either have partners discuss their experiences
with each other; or, when time is limited, ask that
people listen while you describe the next part.

Part 2   In the same dyads, A makes a short
               statement about something he or
she believes is true. B responds verbally to the
statement not by agreeing, disagreeing, or deciding
its validity, but by trying to understand at least
three possible meanings of the statement.
Generally, some meanings are those of which
A was not aware.

The way in which B culls three meanings is
structured. B asks questions beginning with the
words "Do you mean...?" followed by his or
her own ideas of what A might have meant.

A is restricted to three answers: "Yes," "No," and "Partially."

If, after a number of attempts, B is having difficulty getting three yeses, he or she asks A for another version of the statement and then tries again for three yeses.

After explaining this exercise to the group, offer to demonstrate. Ask someone in the group to work with you. Here's an example:

A: I believe that participating in something is more interesting than merely observing.

B: Do you mean you'd rather play a musical instrument than listen to someone else?

A: Yes.

B: Do you mean you wanted me to know you play?

A: No.

B: Do you mean you'd like me to ask you to play something now?

A: No.

B: Do you mean you want to know if I play an instrument, too?

A: Yes.

B: Do you mean you wanted to find out what kinds of things we may have in common?

A: Yes.

As people are doing this exercise, go around the room offering to help. Some people may find it difficult at first to stay within the structure of the exercise.

After the A's have declared three yeses, partners reverse roles. B's now make the starting statement.

Part 3   This part is like the previous one, except that A asks questions instead of making a statement. Responses are the same as in Part 2, i.e., "Do you mean by your question...?" rather than a response to B's question.

Be prepared to demonstrate again if necessary.

A: Do you like this exercise?

B: Do you mean you are uncomfortable with it?

A: Partially.

B: Do you mean you want to know how I feel?

A: Yes.

> **B:** Do you mean you wonder how this exercise applies to what the workshop is about?
>
> **A:** No.
>
> **B:** Do you mean you preferred the others?
>
> **A:** No.

After several more nos:

> **B:** I now need more information in order to ask questions that would help me understand your meanings.

At this point, A rephrases the question and B again tries for three yeses.

After the demonstration, ask the group to begin. As each partner takes one or two turns, again move around the room offering to help, as needed.

Some couples may begin discussions of other subjects in a sharing way. This may be more meaningful for them than repeating the exercise while waiting for others to finish.

Part 4   A begins by quoting a cliché or a proverb. B tries to find at least three meanings by asking questions, again beginning with "Do you mean ...?" After three yeses, partners reverse roles.

You may want to give a demonstration:

    A: The grass is always greener on the other side.

    B: Do you mean you are often attracted by things you don't have?

    A: Yes.

    B: Do you mean you think other people's lives are more fascinating than yours?

    A: Yes.

    B: Do you mean you feel my job is more interesting than yours?

    A: No.

    B: Do you mean you sometimes feel you'd like to have some of the things others have?

    A: Yes.

    B: Do you mean that "wishing for things others have" is a feeling you believe you shouldn't have?

    A: Yes.

Discussion   During this discussion, people usually share life experiences. You may notice that people are more relaxed, candid, trusting, and friendly. Emphasize that it is this manner of phrasing questions that makes this kind of sharing possible.

Flip Chart   Under "What Affects Communication," add:

Asking questions starting with "why"

Requesting (or not requesting) or receiving clarifying information

Being defensive about a conviction, comment, or assertion

Under "Communication Tools," add:

Mirroring

"Do you mean...?"

ACTIVATING
THE INGREDIENTS OF
AN INTERACTION

Purpose   Whenever you assist people to
be more congruent in their ways
of communicating, it's important to understand
the many levels of an interaction that exist between
people, whether evident or not. This exercise
presents a visual and experiential demonstration
of the complexity of factors present whenever
two people meet and interact. It shows that
difficulties can arise simply due to the gaps that
exist in any statement. Many ideas are
unexpressed, not because people want to conceal
anything, but because it is literally impossible
to include everything in any statement. Unless
deliberately and thoughtfully expressed in words,
those parts remain unknown and invisible.

This exercise offers the facilitator a useful tool
to clarify and transcend communication dilemmas.
Understanding the ingredients of an interaction
lets a facilitator intervene in specific ways to
clarify an impasse, block, or breakdown in
communication.

Time   One and a half to two hours

Description   As part of an experiential
                      demonstration that requires
at least eight people, participants analyze the
levels of communication between people who
interact in verbal, nonverbal, and behavioral ways.
Virginia Satir named these levels the *ingredients
of an interaction.*

As you describe the exercise, you can illustrate
these levels on a flip chart. (See the diagram that
follows this list.)

1. Manifestation: The participant A will make
   a statement or ask a question. The second
   participant, B, will not respond.

2. Level of Sensory Input: A third participant,
   representing B's sensory input, will put
   words to anything he or she sees: A's
   expressions, body positions, breathing,
   movements, or gestures; and what he or
   she heard: the words, and the tone and
   pitch of A's voice. This participant reports
   on everything that comes through the five
   senses.

3. Level of Explanation ("Making Meaning"):
   Another participant, representing B's level
   of explanation, will report his or her
   thoughts, explanations, understanding,
   images, and interpretations of what A said.

4. Level of Feelings: A fifth participant, representing B's feelings, will talk about his or her feelings after hearing the people representing levels 2 and 3.

5. Level of Feelings about the Feelings: A sixth person will represent this level. He or she expresses feelings about what the previous participant said. For instance, "You said you felt curious. I never feel it's OK to feel curious." (The implicit idea here is that judging feelings affects our level of self-worth.)

6. Level of Coping: A seventh participant will enumerate the survival rules for reacting to and handling all the preceding feelings and perceptions. What defenses come into play?

   You may want to use this segment to ask about the old survival messages and rules that are the basis for judging a feeling. ("For me, the rule in the family was 'Don't be curious, it isn't polite to pry! No one likes a snoop!' And since I believed my survival in the family depended on their approval, I denied and repressed this feeling. My defense was to become disinterested, and I later discovered that people assumed I just didn't care.")

7. Level of Commenting: An eighth person summarizes B's rules for what she or he

is allowed to say, based on the above
responses.

8. B now responds to A, basing that response
on all the above information. If there is
enough time, B's response can initiate a
similar process, in which A and six
counterparts then react to whatever B said.

After giving this description, ask for any questions
and comments.

The Levels in an Interaction

Interaction	Manifestation	Ingredients
A makes a statement	External (what can be seen and heard)	Words Affect
B perceives and reacts	Internal (what cannot be seen or heard)	Sensory input (what is seen and heard) Meanings and interpretations Thoughts Feelings Feelings about the feelings Survival messages Defenses Rules for commenting
B verbalizes a response	External (what can be seen and heard)	Words Affect

Part 1   Ask for volunteers to represent A,
            B, and B's six levels. A and B stand
next to each other, and B's levels stand beside
B. For example, the person who represents B's
sensory input (what is seen and heard) stands
a little to the side and behind B. Next, B's thoughts
("making meaning") stands behind Sensory Input
and a little to the side. As people are added,
arrange them in a semicircle so that each can see
the others and still be facing the larger group.
(If you are also going to use A's counterparts, ask
them to arrange themselves behind A in a similar
fashion.)

Part 2   Once a semicircle forms, you may
            want a few moments for centering,
            to focus the group.

Begin by asking that A make a statement. Then
follow the procedure described earlier.

Coaching, guiding, and assisting may be necessary
to provoke additional material and to extend
the scope of each response. Sometimes A's
statement elicits only bland feelings. When that
happens, explain that this exercise works best
by eliciting a stronger feeling, and have A alter
the statement accordingly.

At times, participants may detour into a discussion
after one of the parts has spoken. When you want
to resume, sum up what was said previously so
that the focus is clear and people are ready to
move to the next step.

Discussion   Ask each of the volunteer participants to report his or her experiences. Then open up a general discussion with the group.

Flip Chart   Under "Communication Tools," add:

Understanding the ingredients of an interaction

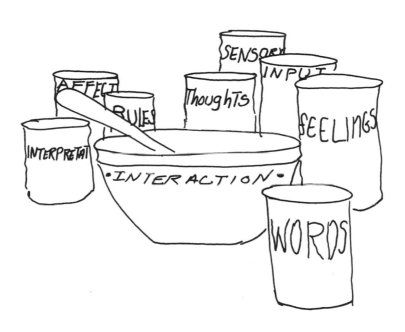

TEMPERATURE TAKING

Purpose   This exercise is a practical way
for a group, family, or company
to check out and focus on the current life
conditions—the what, why, who, when, where,
and how—of its members. It provides a time
and place to exchange essential information, so
each person can truly focus on what is and will be
happening in the group. Equally important, the
exercise allows this to happen in an environment
of discovery: it looks for answers rather than
assessing blame. Normal, ever-present complaints
and concerns are accompanied by several
recommendations for possible solutions.

Overall, it is a tool to create a safe context in
which to make necessary comments, be they
negative or positive. Any group of people can
use this tool to make life together flow more
smoothly.

Time   Fifteen minutes to one hour or more

Description   The group responds to questions
about what the participants
currently need, want, expect, or worry about.
The format described in Part 1 maximizes time,
energy, and goodwill and reduces the possibility
of blame and criticism.

This exercise can be used at the beginning of
any session. It allows everyone to express or obtain
whatever information is needed to be at ease
and comfortable during the session.

Part 1   After explaining the purpose of the
                exercise, describe the following format
and then ask how the group feels about trying
it. As you explain the exercise, write the different
parts on the flip chart.

> *Information:* Does anyone have any
> puzzles or need any information?
> Does anyone have information that
> the group might need?
>
> *Complaints and Recommendations:*
> Does anyone have any dilemmas,
> problems, or complaints? And what
> recommendations do people have
> for solutions?
>
> *Worries and Concerns:* Does anyone
> have any worries or concerns that
> need discussing?
>
> *Appreciations:* Does anyone have
> any appreciations, excitements, or
> wishes to share?

This exercise is especially important at a first
session. It elicits information relevant to the

program and to people's needs, concerns, wishes, hopes, and expectations.

Part 2   Go through each question one by
                  one, taking as much time as needed.
After the discussion, ask what the experience
was like. It's essential that a "temperature taking"
be done slowly and carefully, giving everyone
who wishes to speak the opportunity.

Flip Chart   Under "Communication Tools,"
                   add:

                   Temperature taking

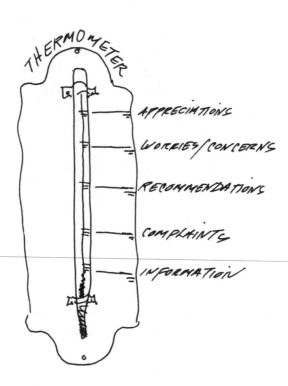

TRANSFORMING RULES

Purpose   Rules that we have about how to speak, behave, feel, or relate to others affect the way we communicate. Some rules prevent us from freely expressing our thoughts and feelings. This exercise makes rules apparent and encourages moving from a rule that imposes restrictions or immobility to one that is flexible and human. Instead of trying to eliminate the rule entirely, this exercise illustrates how to transform it into a realistic statement that can be comfortable and valuable.

Time   Fifteen to thirty minutes

Description   Our behavior or feelings sometimes interfere with talking freely. Often we have "rules" about what we should and shouldn't say. When we find ourselves too constricted for comfort, though, we can identify the rule that seems to be the block and begin to clarify and transform it.

To "hear" a rule, listen for these words:

always

never

should

must

ought

They can clue us in that we are probably responding more to the rule than to the situation.

Part 1   Ask for a volunteer who is willing to work with one of his or her rules that is interfering with communication. Engage the volunteer in conversation until you detect the block. In one sentence, state the rule you believe is present. Check out if that is what the person believes is his or her rule. Again ask if the person is willing to continue this experience of transforming the rule, and ask how he or she feels about doing that.

After clarifying the rule, write it on the flip chart. Ask how he or she feels about seeing the rule as written, and if this is exactly what was meant. If not, modify the statement as many times as necessary to be certain that it is exactly what that person means.

When it reads precisely as the person intends, ask how the person now feels, seeing his or her rule. Again find out if he or she wants to continue transforming the rule and how he or she feels about doing that.

In a step-by-step process, ask the person to add, delete, or substitute one or several words, forming a new sentence each time. Cross out the words that are deleted and add the new ones. Then write the revised version underneath the old sentence.

After the first change, ask the person how he or she feels about the change and whether the new sentence is something he or she can accept and live with. If so, continue the same procedure, adding or deleting words. Write each revision under the last one.

When you reach the point at which that person is no longer comfortable with further changes, ask how the revised rule now feels and what the experience was like. It's important to stop when a person reports that he or she is now comfortable with the amended rule, even though you may see other possibilities. That person may not be ready or able to accept, or have a need for, further changes.

The following is an example of rule transformation:

>*Rule:* "I must always take care of others."

>*Ensuing transformations:*

>I CAN take care of others.

>I can take care of others WHEN IT FITS FOR ME.

I can take care of others when
it fits for me AND THEM.

I can take care of MYSELF.

I can take care of myself and
others when it fits for me and
for them.

Discussion   Have a general discussion, asking
what the experience was like
and whether anyone else would like to transform
one of his or her rules.

Note: You can use this exercise during any session
when you believe a rule is in effect, out of the
person's awareness, and would be usefully
transformed for that person.

Flip Chart   Under "Communication Tools,"
add:

Rule Transformation

Appendices

APPENDIX 1

Sample Charts

What Affects Communication

Position

Comfort level

Changes: *in places*
in group size or
membership
in body position
in time

Rules: *for feelings*
for behavior
for communication

for how to treat others
for how to respond to
    others
for dealing with
    differences

Use of indirect pronouns

Use of direct pronouns

Old survival rules

Old survival feelings

Certain words and phrases

Projections

Stress and the different
communication responses to stress

Decision making

Planning

Assumptions, preconceptions

Stereotypes

Prejudices

Rumors

Asking questions beginning with
"Why"

Feelings of: *having to conform*
taking risks
being interrupted
interrupting
being left out
being included
being excluded
going into new
     situations
separating
leaving
ending
saying good-bye
relief
being discriminated
     against
being ignored
being abandoned

Being one of a triad

Trying to break into an ongoing
situation

Moving back into one's original
connection or group

Having to incorporate a new
person into an existing situation

Being introduced into new groups

Creating new groups of people

Making decisions about leaving or
staying with a situation

Being observed by others

Feeling responsible for the comfort
of others

Being defensive about a conviction,
comment, or assertion

Communication Tools

Sculpting the communication
positions

Rule transformation

Temperature taking

Mirroring: "Do you mean ...?"

Activating the ingredients of an
interaction

Your experiences in the workshop

APPENDIX 2

The Five Freedoms
by Virginia Satir

The freedom to see and hear what
is here instead of what should be,
was and/or will be

The freedom to say what one feels
and thinks instead of what one should

The freedom to feel what one feels
instead of what one ought to feel

The freedom to ask for what one wants
instead of waiting for permission

An artistic poster using these words is available through
Celestial Arts, P.O. Box 7327, Berkeley, CA 94707.

The freedom to take risks in one's behalf instead of wanting only to be secure

In these statements, Virginia Satir expressed her belief that people can live more fully and creatively—and develop more satisfying relationships—when they live the Five Freedoms. An integral part of her teaching, they reflect her basic philosophy that every person can learn and grow.

In addition to using words in her workshops, Virginia Satir demonstrated the crippling effect of denying a person the freedom to see, hear, and move. She would ask for volunteers and then use scarfs to cover their eyes, ears, and mouth, and tie ropes around their feet and hands. This dramatizes the many ways we subtly limit our resources for living more productive, growth-filled, creative, and satisfying lives.

Appendix 3
Suggested Equipment

Tape recorder, tapes, and batteries

Extension cord and three-way plug

Adhesive tapes (scotch, masking, strapping)

Ball of string

Rubber bands

Scissors

Paper clips

Extra pens, marking pens, crayons

Flip chart

Notebook

Swiss army knife

Facial tissues, premoistened towelettes

Handouts: copies of diagrams, literature, your cards, etc.

For Avanta materials, Satir publications, and dates of other workshops, write:

Avanta Network
139 Forest Street
Palo Alto, California 94301

APPENDIX 4

Practice Suggestions

The following exercises are especially well suited to practice independently with friends, family, or other group members:

Temperature taking

Rule transformation

"Do You Mean...?"

Mirroring

Sculpting

Using direct, personal pronouns

Paying attention to comfort and body position while talking

People can find more extensive descriptions of these and other exercises in Virginia Satir's book *The New Peoplemaking* (Palo Alto, California: Science and Behavior Books, Inc., 1988).

About the Authors

Johanna Schwab, MSW/ACSW/LCSW, began studying with Virginia Satir in 1962, was a founding member of the Avanta Network, and continued her professional and personal relationship until Satir's death in 1988. Schwab has been in private practice since 1970 in Los Angeles and is also active as a consultant and lecturer. She is presently an Adjunct Clinical Associate Professor at the University of Southern California Graduate School of Social Work and was formerly Director of Family Therapy at the Westwood Mental Health Clinic.

Michele Baldwin, PhD/MSW/MFC, studied with Satir beginning in 1969 and was a founding member of the Avanta Network. She is now a trainer at the Virginia Satir International Training Institute. In 1983 she and Satir coauthored the book *Satir Step by Step: A Guide to Creating Change in Families.* She is currently Assistant Professor of Clinical Psychiatry and Behavioral Sciences at Northwestern University School of Medicine and practices marital and family therapy in Chicago.

Jane Gerber, MSW/ACSW, has been a trainer at the Satir Institute since 1981 and is a former member of the Avanta Network Governing Council. She cofounded and is new vice president of the Oasis Midwest Training Center, and Fellow and senior faculty member of the Gestalt Institute of Chicago. She also practices psychotherapy in Evanston, Illinois.

Maria Gomori, MSW, is a trainer at the Satir Institute and an Assistant Professor in the department of psychiatry at the University of Manitoba's medical school. She lectures at the University of Winnipeg, University of Oklahoma, and in Europe, South America, and Hong Kong.

Virginia Satir (1916-1988) was a pioneer in family therapy, recognized internationally for her special warmth and powerful ideas about human communication and self-esteem. A prolific author, lecturer, and trainer of others in the helping professions. With these colleagues and many more, she founded the Avanta Network in 1977.

THE AVANTA NETWORK

Virginia Satir founded her Avanta Network to teach methods for enhancing the process of change and improving human relations. Its 160 members worldwide are colleagues who studied, worked, and shared with Virginia over the years. Their Avanta work reflects her goals of developing a consciousness toward peace, individual health, and social and personal responsibility.

Activities of the Network include the annual four-week Process Community training program in Crested Butte, Colorado, advanced training for Process Community graduates, and workshops across North America and throughout the world.

For more information about the Network or the Virginia Satir International Training Institute (including the Process Community), write to Avanta Network, 139 Forest Avenue, Palo Alto, CA 94301.

For Your
Notes and Ideas